ILD ABOUT CATS!

Lions

by Alicia Z. Klepeis

BLASTOFF! READERS 3

BELLWETHER MEDIA • MINNEAPOLIS, MN

Blastoff! Readers are carefully developed by literacy experts to build reading stamina and move students toward fluency by combining standards-based content with developmentally appropriate text.

Level 1 provides the most support through repetition of high-frequency words, light text, predictable sentence patterns, and strong visual support.

Level 2 offers early readers a bit more challenge through varied sentences, increased text load, and text-supportive special features.

Level 3 advances early-fluent readers toward fluency through increased text load, less reliance on photos, advancing concepts, longer sentences, and more complex special features.

★ **Blastoff! Universe**

Reading Level

Blastoff! Beginners — Grade K

Blastoff! Readers — Grades 1–3

Blastoff! Discovery — Grade 4

This edition first published in 2024 by Bellwether Media, Inc.

Library of Congress Cataloging-in-Publication Data

LC record for Lions available at: https://lccn.loc.gov/2023046600

Editor: Betsy Rathburn Designer: Brittany McIntosh

Printed in the United States of America, North Mankato, MN.

Table of Contents

Family Pride

Lions are big cats with loud roars. They live in grasslands, open woodlands, and areas of thick brush.

Lions are very **social**. They live in **prides**.

Most lions live south of the Sahara Desert in Africa. A small number live in India.

Lions are **vulnerable**. Their numbers are dropping. This is mostly because of **habitat** loss and hunting.

Mighty Manes

Lions have tan coats. Their long tails have dark fur at the end. Adult males have **manes**.

Lions have sharp, **retractable** claws and long **canine** teeth. These help them hold on to **prey**.

Identify a Lion

Lions can reach over 8 feet (2.4 meters) long. Their tails can add another 3 feet (0.9 meters) or more!

Size Comparison

house cat	lion
height at shoulder	**height at shoulder**
around 10 inches (25 centimeters)	around 48 inches (122 centimeters)
length (without tail)	**length (without tail)**
around 18 inches (46 centimeters)	over 96 inches (244 centimeters)

Females weigh up to 400 pounds (181 kilograms). Males weigh over 500 pounds (227 kilograms).

Night Hunters

Lions rely on their pride. A pride can have up to 40 members. Most are female.

Pride members work together. Males **defend** their **territory**. Females raise the young.

Females do most of the hunting.
They often hunt together.
They usually hunt at night.

Lions sneak up on prey. Then, they chase it! Lions can reach 50 miles (80 kilometers) per hour!

Lions are **carnivores**. They hunt many kinds of prey. They also steal food from other animals.

Favorite foods include zebras, wildebeests, antelope, and buffalo. Male lions can eat about 140 pounds (64 kilograms) of meat at once!

Lion Diet
zebras
wildebeests
buffalo

Lion Litters

Lion **litters** usually have two to four cubs. Mothers give birth away from the pride. Mothers and cubs stay away for four to six weeks.

The cubs grow and get stronger. Then they join the pride.

Baby Lions

name for babies: cubs
time with mom: life (females); around 2 years (males)

Moms teach their cubs to hunt. Cubs learn to **stalk** and **pounce**.

Female cubs stay with their mom's pride. Males leave when they are around two years old. Within a few years, they join a new pride!

In the Wild

habitats:

grasslands

open woodlands

areas of thick brush

conservation status: vulnerable

Least Concern	Near Threatened	**Vulnerable**	Endangered	Critically Endangered	Extinct in the Wild	Extinct

population in the wild: around 20,000

population trend: going down

life span: up to 16 years

Glossary

canine—related to the long, pointed teeth that are often the sharpest in the mouth

carnivores—animals that only eat meat

defend—to keep safe

habitat—a land area with certain types of plants, animals, and weather

litters—groups of babies that are born at the same time

manes—thick rings of hair that grow around male lions' faces

pounce—to suddenly jump on something

prey—animals that are hunted by other animals for food

prides—groups of lions that live and travel together

retractable—able to be pulled back in

social—living in groups

stalk—to hunt slowly and quietly

territory—the land area where an animal lives

vulnerable—at risk of becoming endangered

To Learn More

AT THE LIBRARY

Bodden, Valerie. *Lions.* Mankato, Minn.: Creative Education, 2020.

Markarian, Margie. *Lions.* Washington, D.C.: National Geographic Kids, 2023.

Williams, Tyus D. *Big Cats: What Do Lions, Tigers, and Panthers Get Up to All Day?* New York, N.Y.: Neon Squid, 2022.

ON THE WEB

FACTSURFER

Factsurfer.com gives you a safe, fun way to find more information.

1. Go to www.factsurfer.com.
2. Enter "lions" into the search box and click 🔍.
3. Select your book cover to see a list of related content.

Index

The images in this book are reproduced through the courtesy of: Eric Isselee, front cover (lion), pp. 3, 9, 11 (lion), 19 (cub), 23; Volodymyr Burdiak, front cover (background), p. 4; KenCanning, p. 5; alihrdinova, p. 6; Maggy Meyer, pp. 8, 16-17; PACO COMO, pp. 10-11; Nynke van Holten, p. 11 (house cat); Reto Buehler, p. 12; Lisa Hagan, p. 13; Fernando Castelani, p. 14; Catchlight Lens, p. 15; Amitrane, p. 16; Amelandfoto, p. 17 (zebra); nwdph, p. 17 (wildebeest); Rudi Hulshof, p. 17 (buffalo); AzizAlbagshi, p. 18; Dave Pusey, p. 19 (inset); Dr Ajay Kumar Singh, p. 20; brytta, pp. 20-21.